Standing Stones

New & Collected Poems

poems by

Robert René Galván

Finishing Line Press
Georgetown, Kentucky

Standing Stones

New & Collected Poems

ACKNOWLEDGMENTS

I am grateful to the following publications and their editors, where versions
of these poems have found homes:

Abstract Elephant	"And so I went to Peter's well"
Arachne Press Limited	"Dominion"
Arthropod Literary Journal	"Ancestors"
Burningword Literary Journal:	"Words"
From Sac	"North Shore"
Inkwell Journal	"Perennials"
Newtown Literary	"Grand Central"
Phantom Kangaroo	"Sasquatch"
Public Poetry— *Pandemic Anthology*	"Nature's lovely face belies her terror"
Right Hand Pointing	"I've lost the last line…"

Publisher: Leah Huete de Maines
Editor: Christen Kincaid
Cover Photo and Design: Robert René Galván
Author Photo: Holly Hepp-Galván

Order online: www.finishinglinepress.com
also available on amazon.com

Author inquiries and mail orders:
Finishing Line Press
P. O. Box 1626
Georgetown, Kentucky 40324
U. S. A.

Table of Contents

for Morris Beachy

"We are a landscape of all we have seen."

Isamu Noguchi

Words

From time
immemorial
we've pressed them
into clay,
or stone,
a coarse brush
of ochre
on cave walls,
engravings
on sarcophagi
and on forgotten
stelae
consumed
by the greedy
jungle;
they've flowed
from tributaries
of indigo
on the odd leaf
of skin,
or pulp,
from feathered
quills,
or styli
of steel:
enough pages
to fill the oceans,
letters raised
on the road
rash of billboards,
a forest of graffiti:
the legacy
of pictographs
and glyphs,
cursive and kanji,
cuneiform sagas
and the enigmatic

runes,
Sanskrit scriptures
that whisper across
millennia,
the Aleph
and the Roman
dispersed
through the staccato
music of keys
that sing
through a conduit
of light,
engulfs
the world
to convey
a mere
shadow
of meaning.

North Shore

The great stone
stands alone,
unmoved
since the glacier's
retreat,
the rocky beach
glistens
in the low tide
and treasures
abound
in the lull:
shells of horseshoe
crabs litter
the shore
like the armor
of fallen
angels
and a meteorite
burnished
by waves
stands out
against
a mosaic
of glass
and
half-worn
bottles,
gnarled
driftwood
and shards
of wrecked
ships,
a felled
eagle's
scant feathers,
the delicate
architecture

of bones
exposed,
pinions
still poised
for flight;
we too stride
here for
a time
at the pleasure
of the moon,
her face scarred
by errant stones
from a distant
sea.

Perennials

In the barren
garden,
a few spears
in advance
of the daylily,
mint peers
cautiously
into the tepid
air,
urns stare
at the sky,
with last
spring's
soil spent
on annuals;
an empty
seashell
sings
the memory
of the wave,
draws the starling
to homestead
beneath
the awning -
crocus,
dianthus,
sage,
all return
in their own
time,
coaxed
by a lonely
star.

Cathedral

Each morning,
I gather the fallen
Stones of dreams,
Or blocks from the mind's
Deepest quarries,
Or the remnants
Of earlier ruins
To erect arches
In defiance of gravity.

Labyrinthine corridors
And myriad galleries
Form a vast chasm
For my own echo;

I sing in the darkness.

Perhaps my follies
Are doomed
To fall under
Their own weight,
Engulfed by tendrils,
A fractured architecture
Found by the odd
Wanderer.

Brompton Cemetery, London

I.

Scattered on the grass
Among the dead,
The living lunch
Under the rare March sun.

A silent census retreats
Like a cascade of tiles,
The most distant names
Burnished into anonymous stone.

Carriage wheels sing,
A jogger darts,
Old men read the paper
And play chess—
The incense of cigarettes.

There is no hush here;
The dead do not wake.

II.

The sculptor lies with his sons
Who waited for him beneath the stone
Chiseled by his grief.

A sapling he sowed in sorrow
Now sprawls to an enormous embrace,
Gathers the shades into leaves
That sip the delicious warmth
Of the sun.

Nature's lovely face belies her terror

Nature's lovely face
belies her terror;

a shrug of warm air,
and the dogwood
bursts into snowy
laughter,
the underground
erupts into yellow
corollas
when the earth
shudders
and the hive
arises from a single
sleeper;
the frog's golden
eye peers
from the mud;

Gaia reclines,
the forest hoists
its sails to catch
the star,
and we are seduced
by its luminous
smile,

while underfoot
a silent plexus
does its terrible
work,
generations multiply,
find their way to us
on tattered wings
indifferent
to our joy.

Pandora

Because we could not let the forest rest,
an Armageddon of trees ensues,
a mosaic of bats
flees into the deep thicket,
the howlers retreat,
fling dung at the invaders
as great spades release
the sleeping
spirits of the loam;
they will seek vengeance
unseen,
stowaway spores
on unknowing
voyagers
for we have opened
the box
to the four corners.

Grand Central—March 2020

The terminal
stands empty
like a ruined
temple
of Piranesi's;
rain plays
its mantra
upon the dome,
an absent
throng
persists
somewhere
in the cavern
of tiles,
echoes
of lives,
memories
that wash
over each other
like a dream
that wanes
with waking.

Hart Island

A forgotten archipelago
on the sound
but for the coming
and going
of Charon's barge,
a procession
of the forgotten,
no coins to grace
their lifeless eyes,
a grim inventory
stowed in trenches,
the beloved
lost among the many,
so many.

Astoria Ferry

*And you that shall cross from shore to shore years hence are more to
me, and more in my meditations, than you might suppose.*
—Walt Whitman

I tried to write this poem with a feather, but the words were too heavy;
I wanted to feel the ink bleed onto the page as it did so many years ago.

Instead, I filled my fountain pens, gathered my tomes,
and boarded a ferry on the East River, rode on the upper deck,
the benevolent sun on my face, the wind promising
to launch my hat like a kite.

The craft edged past the slow progress of barges and tugs;
The river requires of us a patience that is now in short supply.

The aluminum ray knifed past a lighthouse at the tip of a slender island,
First stop under the massive ribs of the Queensborough Bridge and the
groaning cables of the tramway, then past the ruined asylum consumed by
vines, difficult to leave the atrium of linden trees, the white granite frame
where a great bronze face mourns in silence.

As the vessel zagged from shore to shore, I tried to imagine steamboat
paddles slapping the water, or the Siwanoy launching their hollowed trunks
into the estuary, long before asphalt arteries fed the city's massive heart.

As we passed the very first bridge, I tried to read the old bard's words
etched in steel near the shore where he often crossed and mused about the
multitudes to come, lines written years before the towers rose like
cathedral vaults.

Onward to the tip of what had been Mannahatta, now a vast hub, confluence
of ocean and river, land and sky: the plexus of streets converge from the
north, round off at the shore: helicopters buzz like dragonflies, great ships
arrive from Europe and ferries still depart to all the islands: Governor's,
Liberty, Brooklyn, and Staten Island:

I once had a dream where I entered the glass façade of the Staten Island Ferry, the mall completely empty. I ascended the escalator and walked through the massive doors into the light, toward an unknown destination.

Man-of-War

An opaque wing
of amethyst and opal,
toxic tendrils trail
like varicose veins,
gather the sea
with a chorus of cells,

bound together
by electric waves,
not a neuron
among them
to drift on the whims
of the wind,

to live,
to be.

Territopsis dohrnii

Delicate medusa—
       unfurls from a planula,
              opens like a dandelion
                     to the whims
                            of the sea:
                     crown of luminous filaments
              translucent ballast,
       with no brain to question itself
or look beyond the moment,
       but electric and persistent,
              suspended
                     in the pure
                            buoyancy
                                   of being:
                                          immortality.

The Pickle Jar

Every year, Mr. D would open the cabinet
where the boy slept,

Preserved before his first breath,
still wrapped around himself
like a coiled frond,

Fingerprints unfurled,
lips pursed to suckle,
but not destined to live,
nor to descend to anonymity of ash,

But to dream in a jar of brine,
his patina fading in the darkness,

Someone's unborn son.

Butterfly in my Brain

It fills its sails
with fluid of flight,
feeds on my senses,
grows dense
in the dark nest
of my mind.

Poised to rend
the strands
of dreams,
it will soar
when it no longer
needs my flesh.

Dominion

Who can say how the Weaver Bird
Builds his mansion
From a thousand blades of grass,
The warp and weft
Of his ebony beak
For the prospect of love;

Or how the foal unfolds
From her wet heap
And trembles to her feet,
Ready to take her place
In the field of thistles
And wild yarrow;

Or how the tadpole evades
The mandibles of the dragonfly larva,
Unaware that he will soon become
A frog and exact revenge
With his darting tongue;

Or how the lumbering leatherback,
An angel in the water,
Returns to the same sand
To bury her clutch year after year,
Or how the egret knows
When the feast will hatch on the shore;

Or how the hornet's silo
Emerges from saliva and pulp
And from a pair of ganglia,
And likewise, the host
Of butterflies navigate
a continent from a bundle
In the thorax;

And how our own pale progeny
Arrive writhing and helpless
To assume dominion.

Fukushima

A ring of white pagodas
Where the land meets the sea,
Unwisely poised upon a fracture,
Feeds a city of light
From dimensions
We can barely perceive,

But the earth shutters,
Folds the vast waters
Into an angry arch,
With such force that it shifts
On its spine,
The island plunged
Into darkness,
And at once
Thousands lost.

When the flood recedes,
A single tree stands
Near the cracked domes,
The village, a habitation
Of wild boar
And feral cats,
A cascade of atoms
Bleeds into the tide.

The catastrophe
Seems so distant
From our shore,
But years pass,
The rift still rent,
Toxic spores migrate
With the current,
Disrupt acidic gyres,
Unwind into warped
Butterflies,
And dolphins marooned
On the sand.

Grind

We have placed
our faith
in the machine,
a trust
as errant
as that
for the temple;
mesmerized
by singing
gears,
we eat an apple
riddled
with worms,
insidious
shoots
ingrained,
oblivious
to what was
taken from us,
perception
parsed
into minute
flakes,
invisible storms
in the ether,
measured,
quantified,
crudely
verified,
the largest
among them
festers
in a Swiss
hole,
groans
in its vast
coils,

retreats
to eternity
and finds
only
an ineffable
mind.

And so I went to Peter's Well

"There's that lovely old Austrian folk song: "The dear cattle need water, fallera, falleri," if you remember. Water is of course the most important raw material we have today in the world. It's a question of whether we should privatize the normal water supply for the population. And there are two different opinions on the matter. The one opinion which I think is extreme, is represented by the NGOs, who bang on about declaring water a public right. That means that as a human being you should have a right to water. That's an extreme solution."
                                               -Peter Brabeck-Latmathe, former CEO of Nestlé

We are spun from the elements,
A sack of minerals but for the dance
Of atoms that made the rain;

It has graced the clouds,
Kissed the mountains,
Wrought the sea that lives
In our veins—

A mystic music we divine
With a rod, collect to cisterns,
Race though aqueducts,
Hoard in great towers.

Entire civilizations have fallen
Bereft of it.

Wasser braucht das liebe Vieh,
Fallera, falleri! *

From a pristine fortress in the Alps,
A suit proclaims that we have no
Human right to water,
That everything must have a price
Just as he has his.

Wasser braucht das liebe Vieh,
Fallera, falleri!

He leads a global bememoth
That stalks indigenous springs
To drain and sell back for profit.

Chilean peasants are arrested
For gathering the storm,
The Guarini threatened.

Und jetzt gang i ans Peters Brünnele….**

We fear armies of annihilation,
But under our noses,
An avuncular pitchman,
A happy clown,
And a cheerful song:

Wasser braucht das liebe Vieh,
Fallera, falleri!

We may well die of thirst.

Fallera, falleri!

---

*The dear cattle need water, fallera, falleri.
  From the Austrian folksong, *Wasser ist zum Waschen da*

***And so I went to Peter's well*, title of an Austrian folksong

Totem

The monolith towers over the trees,
Thrusts towards clouds,

Benign expression of the great face,
Inviting, tempting….

Millennia from now when voracious roots
Have consumed the road,

They will come to worship with offerings
Of herbs and spices—

Eleven.

Murrain

The sulfurous moon
draws denizens
of the sod,
germs
from their
cold cells;
the crocus
sends its green
tongue
through a corpse
of leaves
as if to sing
past winter's
dirge
and angels
of the air
return to the worm
from the bluest
of skies
over empty
streets;
the sudden
warmth belies
a tremor
beneath,
a scourge
from the East;
it's tendrils
embrace
the world.

Skull—*F. catus*

She found it on a pyre of leaves in the forest,
Poised as if it were an offering to the wood spirits,
The pallor of the moon,
Its meager brain carried off by ants.

At first, we thought it to be a raccoon's, or a possum's,
But no mistaking the nocturnal orbits,
Or the temporal bones.

Perhaps it gave up one of its lives
To the hunger of a fox,
Curiosity unabated by fear.

The Calf

She glides from her mother's inner ocean
As easily as changing a garment,
Enters the vast sea,
Rises toward the sun for her first breath,
Unfettered by gravity, nor by the machine,
But suspires and sings.

Sasquatch

You'll never find me;

I inhabit the realm
between imagination
and fear,
denizen of the dark
world,
of vast pines
and
Himalayan
climbs,
 a shadow
in the timberline,
a ghost in the snow.

The First Peoples
knew me,
left offerings
at the edge
of the village,
but you follow
me against
my desire,
gather tufts
of hair,
cast enormous
footprints
in the mud;

I will retreat
deeper into
oblivion
until there are
no more trees.

Shaving

I look into the glass
and the ape
stares back,
brow softened
by millennia
of progressive grace,
the eyes self-aware,
nostrils still flared,
vestigial fangs
bared to a brush;
the blade tuned
on a strap
strips bristles
from the face
as if to erase
the beast
which somehow
lurks there
and cannot
be trusted.

Ancestors

A rift in the Songline—

The persistent mantra
falls silent,
voice of the heat itself
blown from hollow
branches
and the lips
of stone faces,
the Dreamtime
drawn to an alternate
world of pallid beings
that they supposed
to have been spirits,
that they painted
themselves
the color of death,
encountered
the interlopers,
the Empire's
forsaken,
bringers of
concrete
and the detritus
of civilization,
feral cats
and insidious
toads,
the doom
of fantastical
creatures,
and the first
peoples
trapped inside
the loom,
or banished
to the edge

of the red clay
as if they had
never existed.

Standing Stones

For Morris Beachy

The row of stones he laid
On his path to the sea
Lies obscured by the haze of spray
And the approaching squall.

As stelae begin to fall behind him,
The way back is lost
In a rubble of forgetfulness;

The grey shale shore engulfs
Origin and journey,
Renders the code, so keenly etched,
Unintelligible.

No longer lithe, he must stagger
To the void where the land meets the sea,
And when the last slab topples into sand,
He will simply forget to breathe.

The Old Oak

for James Hepp

His grey eyes gaze
at the amber sound,
close like tulips for the night
as the fountain sings
in the last light.

When the boy
first landed here
there was nothing
but the stubborn cliff,
a glacial stone in the tide,
a stand of locusts
before the sapling
reached for the sun,
embraced generations
of birds, hid a child
in its arms:

He grew to see it felled
by a vast and relentless
storm, a maple in its stead,
scarlet sails scattered
like vague memories
of green.

The Stranger

I peer through windows,
gaze at the warm light.

Sometimes I sit inside
surrounded by the music
of laughter,
words rising
and bursting
like bubbles,

But I can never stay;
always drawn beyond
drapes and over sills,
a waft of song
in the night air.

On his birthday....

He gratefully gathers
stray strands
of summer
transgressed
into the amber
Autumn light,

Drinks in the last
bright hues
like elixir
before the asters
seal themselves
into seed.

Wild yarrow,
bitter on the fingertips,
he presses to his face
and lips
as if to fix fast
the memory
of having lived.

Barbers

First, there was Slim,
Who had a small shop on the square
Where I waited beneath a swirling candy cane
For him to grudgingly trim my coarse, black locks
With angry electric shears as if I were a sheep,
And scrunched with Vitalis
So that I looked like a hedgehog,
Which was considered a "decent" cut.

Eventually, Lamar replaced Slim,
But we went instead to Enrique,
A man with ancient eyes,
Who smelled of Barbasol and Tres Flores
Brilliantine, looked more like a dentist
In his white smock, who spoke in low,
Measured tones to my father about politics
And literature, gave me Mexican comic books
And Jarritos while I waited my turn
When the clippers sang in my ears
And his gentle hands massaged pomade
Into my scalp.

Now, Sal washes my strands as he sings
A quiet song in his throat,
His insistent fingers soften all worries
And he sculpts my pate with a razor,
Careful to maintain the pouf
With a fragrant gel.

Still, no one as expert as my mother
With the golden scissors from her sewing kit,
Trimmed with deft gestures as if shaping
A topiary, finished with Johnson's Baby Oil
And a slender comb, stepped back to admire
Her work and sighed:

"Que lindo, mijo."

From a Dream Journal….

The mamba's obsidian coil,
delirium in its jaws,
watches over me
on the mantle
of the couch
where I fell asleep.

In its absence
I awake,
search the empty house;

You peer from a crack
in the bathroom door,
wear a mask
from *Lucha Libre,*
towel wrapped
around your wet hair
like a turban—

I wander out
into the despondent
night.

Inertia

I am tethered
to the world
by time;
even in the vast
abyss
of this
moment
I cling
to the moorings
of the past,
mystic
chords/cords
that feed
the instrument,
strands
rent
by the insistent
stroke
of the future,
forced into
a cluster
of disparate
tones.

Waiting Room

Blemished by the searing sun,
They emerge from the white door,
       a patch on the forehead, the nose,
       the bare pate.

The surgeon, bedecked like a high priest,
       a teal smock and gloves,
          the kufi and mask,

Propitiates Apollo with small offerings of flesh—

His chariot races across the sky,
In its wake, shards of life and death.

I've lost the first line

I've lost the first line
of this poem, or, possibly, the last.

It lingers like a phantom limb—
I sense it, but can't take the first step
because it isn't there.

Portent

The world is bathed
in an eerie amber light,

a heat that lingers like
an unwelcome guest;

a storm looms in the distance
like the end of the world.

Anno

What's a year in the vast arm of the storm,
The eddies' curling shell, the migration of the star
and its shimmering orbs?

I sit still and pluck strings that arc into silence,
Trace the song billions of miles from where it began.

MMXVII

How little we've traversed
In the circumference of a year
Tethered as we are to old assumptions
And fears,

The dark days ahead belied
By a façade of lights and the illusion
Of song,

The wisest among us trampled
By the multitudes' rush toward
Their own demise;

I cannot see my own shadow,
Nor hear my own voice.
Who will save this world?

The Turning

A year, our meager measurement,
    closer to the end of the world,
        though I will expire long before
    the Sun's swelling,
        or Wormwood's strike
            from the darkness,
     eternal visitor, persistent ice
        that skirts the sun with its plumage,
          periodic Phoenix,
        its moment of truth
          in the release of its tether:

  galaxies consume each other,
     suns explode into disembodied
         fields, vast and amoebic,
      congeal back to orbs
          of gas and stone;

      spheres sing in the void
        as Kepler imagined,
          the intonation of cosmic cords,
            minerals infused with light—

  Life exists within finite borders;
  form gives meaning,
  a brief witness and wonder
  that fades from understanding

as we sleep in the moon's umbra
    after our midnight revels,
        dream of the future,
           deny that even stars
              must die.

The force that spawned the stars

The force that spawned the stars
And gave the minerals breath
Will sweep them away.

We dance on the edge of a storm
Within a storm,
Our footprints raked
By the wake of ages.

As surely as the moon
Wanes into rings,
The sun consumes itself
In rage,

And all the fires that ever burned,
Are quelled by more than silence,
More than darkness,
Vanish in the mirage of time.

Robert René Galván, born in San Antonio, resides in New York City where he works as a professional musician and poet. His previous collections of poetry are entitled, *Meteors, Undesirable: Race and Remembrance*, and *The Shadow of Time*. Galván's poetry was recently featured in *Adelaide Literary Magazine, Azahares Literary Magazine, Burningword Literary Journal, Gyroscope, Hawaii Review, Hispanic Culture Review, Newtown Review, Panoply, Sequestrum, Somos en Escrito, Stillwater Review, West Texas Literary Review,* and *UU World*. He is a Shortlist Winner Nominee in the 2018 Adelaide Literary Award for Best Poem. His work has been featured in several literary journals across the country and abroad and has received two nominations for the 2020 Pushcart Prize and one for Best of the Web. René's poems also appear in varied anthologies, including *Undeniable: Writers Respond to Climate Change* and in *Puro ChicanX Writers of the 21st Century*.